HOW TO BE A SUPERHERO CALLED SELF-CONTROL

2ND EDITION

by the same author

The Kids' Guide to Staying Awesome and In Control 2nd Edition
Lauren Brukner
Illustrated by Rebecca Burgess
ISBN 978 1 80501 758 5
eISBN 978 1 80501 759 2

Self-Control to the Rescue!
Super Powers to Help Kids Through the Tough Stuff in Everyday Life
Lauren Brukner
Illustrated by Apsley
ISBN 978 1 78592 759 1
eISBN 978 1 78450 619 3

Stay Cool and In Control with the Keep-Calm Guru
Wise Ways for Children to Regulate their Emotions and Senses
Lauren Brukner
Illustrated by Apsley
ISBN 978 1 78592 714 0
eISBN 978 1 78450 300 0

The Mindful Magician and the Trip to Feelings Town
Lauren Brukner
Illustrated by Jennifer Jamieson
ISBN 978 1 83997 138 9
eISBN 978 1 83997 139 6

How to Be a Superhero Called Self-Control

2ND EDITION

LAUREN BRUKNER

ILLUSTRATED BY REBECCA BURGESS

Jessica Kingsley Publishers
London and Philadelphia

First published in Great Britain in 2026 by Jessica Kingsley Publishers
An imprint of John Murray Press

1

Front cover image source: Rebecca Burgess.

The fonts, layout and overall design of this book have been prepared according to dyslexia-friendly principles. At JKP we aim to make our books' content accessible to as many readers as possible.

A CIP catalogue record for this title is available from the British Library and the Library of Congress

ISBN 978 1 80501 755 4
eISBN 978 1 80501 756 1

Printed and bound in Great Britain by Bell & Bain Limited

Jessica Kingsley Publishers' policy is to use papers that are natural, renewable and recyclable products and made from wood grown in sustainable forests. The logging and manufacturing processes are expected to conform to the environmental regulations of the country of origin.

Jessica Kingsley Publishers
Carmelite House
50 Victoria Embankment
London EC4Y 0DZ

www.jkp.com

John Murray Press
Part of Hodder & Stoughton Ltd
An Hachette Company

The authorised representative in the EEA is Hachette Ireland,
8 Castlecourt Centre, Dublin 15, D15 XTP3, Ireland (email: info@hbgi.ie)

This book is dedicated to all children, everywhere. Know that you are all superheroes, amazingly powerful, unique, and wonderful just the way you are. My wish for you is to just believe it, mind, heart, and soul.

Contents

Foreword

Trenton's sweet face and bright smile could light up any classroom! He loved music, playing with friends, and creating stories and drawings that showed the magic inside his mind. But Trenton's smile would quickly fade when someone spoke to him about his behavior and the things he did without even realizing it. Trenton wanted so badly to make everyone happy: his teachers, his parents, his friends. His friends grew frustrated when he called out answers without raising his hand, while they waited patiently. The adults at school were disappointed when he didn't follow directions, directions he hadn't even heard because he was busy playing with his shoes. His parents would remind him to focus on what really mattered at school: listening, learning, doing his best. Trenton was trying. Boy, was he trying so hard.

As many teachers do, I struggled to find ways to help Trenton control his impulses and make the choices he so deeply wanted to make. I would sometimes joke with him that I wished I had a magic wand to help him improve his self-control and help him think before he acted. But what Trenton really needed was not magic. What he needed was an understanding that he already had the tools inside him, he just didn't yet have the strategies to unlock them. What I needed was the knowledge and resources to help him find his own superpowers.

Children do not come into this world pre-wired with self-control. It's something they learn from the adults around them. They need us to model it, to teach them strategies, to give them safe spaces to practice, to make mistakes, and to try again. When students are disregulated, unable to manage their bodies, thoughts, and actions, learning becomes painfully difficult. Punishment doesn't teach self-control. Only compassion and teaching do. That is why I am so grateful for this book you hold in your hands. *How to Be a Superhero Called Self-Control* is a gift from Lauren Brukner to children, families, and educators everywhere. She weaves together relatable stories, simple, effective strategies, and practical tips that empower children to unlock the tools they already have within them. She invites both children and adults to embark on the journey of discovery and growth together. She reminds us that teaching self-control is not just possible, it's essential.

In my 27 years as an elementary classroom educator, I wish I'd had this book for Trenton and so many other students like him. I wish I'd had this book for myself as I learned how to lead young learners toward becoming the heroes of their own stories. You now hold that guide. I whole-heartedly encourage you to read it and use it to help the children in your life discover the superheroes they already are.

Felicia Gray
Nationally Award-Winning Educator
PBS Kids Early Learning Champion
Assistant Lecturer, Teachers College, Ball State University

Preface

It is hard to believe that it has been ten years since I wrote this book, my first interactive picture book in the Awesome and In Control series. This book came about from a passion to allow children to truly have autonomy in being able to manage challenging sensory and emotional feelings while utilizing imaginative components paired with the power of choice, thus allowing them to feel "just right" to fully participate in their life across a range of settings.

It is equally important to understand the value of adults in the self-regulation process, to allow our children to self-regulate effectively. This can be accomplished in a variety of forms. We can assist children through co-regulation, that is, by modeling the strategies themselves or by completing the strategy together with the child. We can provide graded support in cuing the child to complete the strategy through verbal reminders and visuals of the strategies, which decrease as mastery develops.

We can integrate self-regulation into daily routines as

parents, therapists, and educators. When we read a story during instruction or on a rug, we may add a footnote: "Wow, the character may be feeling frustrated that they can't go to the party. Maybe they need to use a mantra. What mantra would you choose if you were in that situation?"

It is an honor to bring this second edition of *How to Be a Superhero Called Self-Control* into the world.

PART 1

For Kids

CHAPTER 1

All About Me: Self-Control!

So, I know some famous superheroes. They're pretty cool people. They even take me along when they do cool stuff like swinging across buildings and flying through the air! I've become less scared during the flying parts, mostly by not looking down.

HAPPY HARRY? What? You haven't heard of him? Hmm, I won't tell him. Well, he is super strong, and (shh ... don't tell anybody), we are working together on some of his anger issues so he can feel calm and happy even when things don't go his way.

You must know **LIGHTNING LIZZY!** No? Are you sure? Well, she must be going too fast for you to see her! It's awesome to be able to go at the speed of light to save the world, but I've been helping her slow down a bit when she has a moment.

Hmm, who else of my superhero buddies might you know? Oh, I got it! **STRETCHY SUE!** She can bend and stretch into all kinds of shapes.

Something that I have been helping her with is being a little flexible in her thinking, not just her body! Kind of funny, no? She can bend and flex in all kinds of ways with her arms and legs, but she doesn't like to be flexible when it comes to things like sharing or doing something another person's way!

And then there's me. Yep, that's right, down there. I'm a superhero, too. See the totally awesome cape and mask? Yep. Pretty cool, huh?

My name is **SELF-CONTROL**. Have you heard of me? Maybe not. I'm not in any comics, and I haven't starred in any movies. I'm more of an "on-the-sidelines" kind of hero.

Have you ever been in a situation where you felt a really "yucky" feeling, but you somehow had the strength and control to feel better? Guess what? I may have been there, whispering my secrets to you!

Well, maybe, maybe not. I lose track of all the kids (and grownups) that I help all over the world. It's an exhausting job ... no relaxing at weekends, no vacations, very little sleep ... but somebody's got to do it.

So, here's my job in a nutshell: My superpower is getting kids to feel like super self-control experts! Being able to get rid of any of the sad, mad, worried, wiggly, scared feelings that can pop up day or night, with my simple bag of superpowers.

Now's not the time to be modest. I'm quite the expert. Self-Control is my superhero name, after all! But, my friends, how does this help you?

Frankly, I'm tired. It's getting a little exhausting having to fly to the many situations where I am needed all day, every day across the globe. The first few times—eating gelato in Milan, sushi in Tokyo, and deep-dish pizza in Chicago, all in one day—were quite exciting.

Now, I just want to have some downtime. Maybe I could start sleeping late at the weekends, curled up on the couch with a good book, without the ever-sounding beep of my self-control alarm watch going off every minute or so.

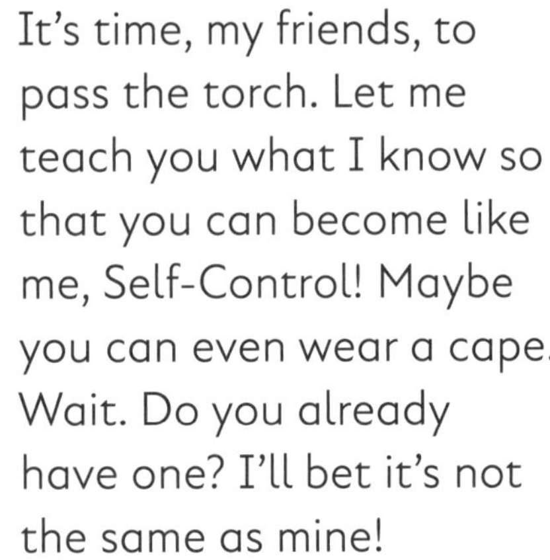

It's time, my friends, to pass the torch. Let me teach you what I know so that you can become like me, Self-Control! Maybe you can even wear a cape. Wait. Do you already have one? I'll bet it's not the same as mine!

CHAPTER 2

How This Book Works

Are you ready to learn how to be a superhero? Great! Put on your cape. Make sure it's nice and tight. Pull it down until it feels just right. Perfect. Now reach deep, deep, deep, into your pocket. Look—there's a mask! Now we are ready to figure out how to help these kids solve their problems and learn my simple bag of superpowers!

It's really kind of magical. Seriously, you don't believe me? You'll see for yourself soon enough. If we do the tip or trick the right way, we help every kid in the world feel like self-control experts!

Are you ready? Thumbs up if you are. OK, let's start!

CHAPTER 3

Frustration

All of the scenes that we are going to look at first have kids who feel frustrated. Do you know what "frustrated" means? When someone feels frustrated, they may feel upset or annoyed, especially if they can't change something or do something the way they want.

Do you have a tip that has worked for you when you felt this way? What made you feel better? If you feel comfortable sharing this, touch your nose quietly. That will show the grownup reading this book that you want to talk about it.

SUPERPOWER #1:
TAKE A DEEP BREATH!

David is playing a board game with his brother. His brother gets the last piece in, to make four in a row. His brother wins the game. Now David is frustrated. He slams the table in frustration and yells, “This is too hard! You always win!”

Let’s learn how to help David feel better together, OK? Go teamwork!

The first power we are going to learn is **Take a Deep Breath!** That's right, a deep breath. But hey, it's harder than it sounds! Let's have some fun with this one!

OK, close your eyes. Pretend that you have a bottle filled with bubbles. Do you feel its weight in your hand? Is it slippery? Make sure to hold onto it tightly! Good. Now, unscrew the cap and pull out the wand. Is it wet? It's OK if it is, just brush it off.

That's called being flexible, which is another awesome self-control thing that we will get to.

Does your bubble wand have enough soap on it? If not, give it another dip in the bubbles. Good, we are all ready.

Now, breathe in slowly through your nose. When you blow out, you are going to blow a bubble as big as the room you are in, as big as the grownup reading this to you. That's pretty big, huh?

Remember, if you breathe too softly, you won't make any bubbles, and if you breathe too fast or too hard, the bubble will pop!

I hope we helped David; board games are fun! It would be a shame if he missed out. Let's turn the page and see...

Yes! **Take a Deep Breath** totally worked! Look at how calm and in control David is. He's really enjoying playing the board game with his brother.

Do you still have your superhero mask on? Great! We're on to our next case.

SUPERPOWER #2: MAKE A MANTRA!

Lily is with her classmates at the arts center. They are drawing pictures of their families. Her hand is hurting, and she doesn't know how to make her picture look like the pictures her friends are drawing. She rips up her picture and throws it in the garbage. Her teacher comes over and asks her why she did that. "I can't draw. My pictures look like scribble scrabble!"

Ready for superpower #2? OK, it sounds kind of funny. It's called **Make a Mantra!** Let's learn how to use it and help Lily feel better together, OK? Go teamwork!

What is that silly "mantra" word? Well, I'll tell you...

When I get frustrated, there are certain words and sentences that I like to tell myself over and over, that make me feel better. For example, if I lose the flying races games at the Superhero Olympics, I tell myself "No big deal!" or "Oh well, maybe next time!"

Why don't you and Lily try it together? Think of something that happened recently that made you feel frustrated. Show a thumbs up when you have that moment in your mind. OK, great! Let's practice saying a few mantras:

Which is your mantra? Show a thumbs up so the adult reading this book knows you have one in your mind. If you want, share it with them.

I hope Lily now feels confident to draw whatever she wants. Even if it's different from the things her friends are drawing. Let's turn the page and see if we helped...

Wow, look at Lily go! **Make a Mantra** has really helped! Lily feels confident and happy with her own drawings. She is making an amazing drawing of her family, even though it's a little different from her friends' pictures.

So you've accomplished your first superhero tasks. You have mastered the first two superpowers: **Take a Deep Breath** and **Make a Mantra** Pat yourself on the back. Great job! You have taken the first two steps to being like me!

SUPERPOWER #3:
USE YOUR WORDS!

Ray is waiting for his turn on the slide. Just as he is about to slide down, another boy pushes him out of the way and slides down first. “Um, um...,” Ray stammers, but, to his frustration, no words come out.

Ray is having trouble using his words. Can you think of a time when you had lots of thoughts and feelings in your head but couldn't explain how you felt? It can be frustrating, can't it?

When you have felt frustrated, have you heard somebody tell you, "Use your words!"? That can feel hard, especially if you are feeling sad, mad, or another kind of bad feeling.

I'll be honest, it is important to use your words to explain how you feel, at least to yourself, and maybe to a grownup who can help you so that you can feel better.

Let's practice the next superpower to help Ray: **Use Your Words!**

Close your eyes, and take a deep breath as we have practiced. Now, I want you to think about how you are feeling at this moment. Are you happy? Peaceful? Tired? Are you frustrated, sad, or angry?

Maybe you are feeling a mixture of many different emotions, and that's OK. When you have your feeling clear in your mind, give a thumbs up. Use your words to tell the adult who is reading this book how you are feeling.

OK, back to Ray. Let's see if using this new superpower, **Use Your Words** has helped Ray. Turn the page and see what we will find...

Awesome work Ray! He used his words to let his friend know how he was feeling. Ray has let his friend know that pushing him aside was unfair and that next time he has to wait for his turn.

Wow! We've helped kids deal with their frustration—great job! Next, we have to power up kids who feel anxious or worried.

CHAPTER 4

Anxiety

Do you know what it means to feel anxious or worried?

When you feel anxious or worried, you may feel nervous about many things. For example, you may feel worried about something that may happen. You may be worried or anxious if you are not sure what to expect.

You may feel worried in your thoughts and also in your body. Your heart may beat quickly. Your stomach may not feel right. Your head may hurt. Other parts of your body may also feel yucky.

Have you ever had the same worrisome thoughts over and over again? Do they pop into your head even when you are trying your best not to think about them? Some kids may try to stay away from people, places, or things that make them feel anxious or worried—but then they are usually missing the best parts of life! Feeling anxious or worried can be tough.

Do you have a tip that has worked for you when you have felt this way? What made you feel better? If you feel comfortable sharing this, touch the top of your head quietly. That will show the grownup reading this book that you want to talk about it.

SUPERPOWER #4:
GIVE YOURSELF A HUG!

Joseph does not like fire drills. Every day, he comes in and asks his teacher, “Are we having a fire drill today?” His teacher is very good at telling him when there will be one so that Joseph can feel less nervous when the loud ringing starts and he has to go with his class down the hallway quickly and line up outside. “It’s just practice,” his teacher reminds him.

One day, the fire alarm rings! Joseph feels so scared! He didn’t hear about it from his teacher. He starts yelling and hides under his desk.

Oh no, we have to get Joseph out of that building and keep him and his class practicing safe fire drill behavior!

Ready for the next superpower? It's one I use myself whenever I get scared. Bunny rabbits are one of those animals that make me scared, OK? Stop laughing! I hear you through the book!

Are you ready? Off we go!

The superpower is ... **Give Yourself a Hug!**

When you feel scared, close your eyes. Think of a place where you feel the most peaceful and happy. Mine is cuddling with my parents under soft blankets on the couch in the living room and sipping hot chocolate.

I picture the softness of the blankets and how cuddly my parents feel, I imagine the sweetness of my hot chocolate on my tongue, and I hear their heartbeats as I lie on their chests.

Back to you. What's your moment? Thumbs up when you've got it. Now, reach out your arms and hug that moment tight so it stays in your heart.

Remember, whenever you feel scared, that moment is right there in your heart. You can always touch your chest, or do this superpower again to feel peaceful so you don't feel scared anymore.

Did **Give Yourself a Hug** help Joseph feel better and get out of the building feeling calm and safe? Turn the page to find out...

Good job, Joseph! Using the power of **Give Yourself a Hug** has calmed Joseph down and he's been able to line up with his class in the hallway! That's a really brave use of that superpower.

OK, great job!

SUPERPOWER #5: CRUMPLE UP YOUR WORRIES!

Lianna is sitting up in her bed, hugging her stuffed bear close and crying. Her sheets are tossed around her. Her hair is in a tangle. Her mom rushes into the room. “Mommy, I had a bad dream! I’m scared!” Her mom rubs her back and whispers, “Go back to sleep, you’re safe.” Lianna just cries louder. “I can’t! I’m just too scared to sleep!”

Do you like to crumple things? I sure do! I love to crumple all types of things: newspaper, construction paper, tissue paper ... you name it. It feels great! You are going to really like our next superpower, **Crumple Up Your Worries!**

Close your eyes. Picture in your mind a piece of paper and a marker. What color is the paper? What color is the marker? In your mind, draw out something that makes you feel scared. Don't leave anything out! You can even scribble scrabble if that makes you feel better!

You can scribble anything you find scary onto the paper. It could be:

- something you've seen like a spider in your room
- a situation you don't like
- a feeling that makes you uncomfortable
- a change in routine.

Now, take your fists and crumple that paper into the smallest ball that you can make. Now, whatever made you worried or scared is gone! You can even put the paper into the basket to keep things tidy.

Let's see if our latest power **Crumple Up Your Worries** helped Lianna fall back asleep. Turn the page and find out...

Great work, Lianna! By using **Crumple Up Your Worries** Lianna has thrown away the thing from her scary dream, and it's not long before she is fast asleep. It's a really neat trick!

Why don't you try it too, the next time you are scared? You can even do it when you are awake if you think of something scary and it will help you forget.

SUPERPOWER #6:
THROW AWAY YOUR WORRIES!

Victor is riding the train with his mom. His ears are ringing, and the sound of the train screeching on the tracks is making his whole body hurt. It is scary. It feels like the noise is coming from inside of him! He covers his ears very tightly, but it just can't block the noise!

"Mom!" His mother rubs his back, hugging him tightly. "It can't hurt you, we are almost off. Don't worry," she says over and over, her voice loud, trying to carry over the screeching of the train. Victor can't hear her words, the noises are just too loud!

Everybody is afraid of something, right? Take me, for example. I'm afraid of teddy bears as well as rabbits. Even Lianna's teddy was scary to me! Hey, I can hear you laughing through the book!

I'm also afraid of loud noises. It's hard for me to go to the movies even though I absolutely love movies. So I definitely understand how Victor feels. Do you?

OK, let's learn a new superpower that can help Victor out. Ready? Let's go!

This superpower is called **Throw Away Your Worries!**

Here's what we are going to do: Look around. Where is a good place that you would want to throw away your worries?

Do you want to throw them out the window? Into the garbage can? Toward the door? What about the back of the chair?

Once you know where you will throw your worries, wiggle your fingers. Now, close your eyes. Where do you feel your worries the most? Are they in your heart? Your belly? Your head? A mixture? What color are your worries? Can you picture them in your mind? Great.

Now, grab your worries from wherever they are, hold onto them, and throw every bit of your worries away to the place that you chose to throw them. Phew. Doesn't that feel better?

Do you think that we helped Victor feel better about the noise on the train? I hope so!

Fantastic work, Victor! Talk about using the right superpower at the right time! Victor has been really brave and used **Throw Away Your Worries** to calm down. He can happily leave the train with his mom. Very cool!

SUPERPOWER #7:
MAKE A WORRY BOX!

Shayna is coming back to school for the first day after winter vacation. She knows her friends in her class, but suddenly she feels afraid to go into the classroom. It just doesn't feel as familiar as it did before she went on winter break.

Her teacher stands by the door: "Welcome back, boys and girls! Come on in!" Shayna's feet feel glued to the floor. She puts her backpack in front of her and starts crying and shaking.

Can I tell you a secret? I don't like coming back to superhero work after I go on short trips and vacations. Parts of my office feel less familiar, less safe. I understand how Shayna feels, don't you? Thumbs up if you understand this feeling.

I'll bet you've had these feelings at times, right? All of us have ... even superheroes.

Let's learn how to help Shayna feel better together, OK? You really are super.

The next superpower we are going to use is called **Make a Worry Box!**

"A what?" you may ask.

That's right, a **Worry Box**. Let's learn how to make one ... in our minds.

Close your eyes. Now, I want you to create a box where you are going to put away all of your worries, anything that you are afraid of, and lock it so that not even one tiny worry can escape. What does your **Worry Box** look like? Is it colorful? Is it smooth or rough? Do you have it in your mind?

Now, put every single drop of anything that's worrying you right now into your **Worry Box** ... make sure to get it all! Carefully close the lid and lock it tightly. Now, those worries are locked away and can't bother us. They're gone!

Do you think that using our **Make a Worry Box** superpower helped Shayna feel safe and happy enough to go into her classroom? Let's find out...

Wow, Shayna, so proud of you! I'm in awe of your superpowers. Using the **Make a Worry Box** superpower means you can be totally chill and relaxed about coming back to school. It's a really great superpower to make you feel a little braver. I think you should try to **Make a Worry Box** whenever something feels strange and unfamiliar.

CHAPTER 5

Sensory Processing

All of the scenes that we are going to look at now have kids who feel wiggly. Do you know what "wiggly" means? When someone feels wiggly, that's their body's way of saying "Hey, I've been sitting still for too long! I need to move!"

Do you have a part of your body where you feel wiggly the most? Some kids do, some kids don't. It's OK, either way. As for me, I usually feel wiggly in my hands and feet. After a while, they just start moving—well, that is, until I do my next super-amazing superpower that you are now going to learn about!

Do you have a tip that has worked for you when you felt this way? What made you feel better? If you feel comfortable sharing this, wiggle your body in your seat. That will show the grownup reading this book that you want to talk about it.

OK, boys and girls. Are you ready to get moving? That's right, we're going to do some exercise. Flex our muscles. Stretch our bodies. And do you want to know why? Of course, you do. It's because these superpowers, my super friends, are specially designed to help kids who need to get out their wiggles in super-fun and super-simple ways!

SUPERPOWER #8: PUSH YOUR WIGGLES!

It is time for a morning meeting in class. Ron is sitting on his rug spot, along the perimeter of the rug. He is trying so very hard to keep his body still, but it's just too hard! His back and neck are hurting, and his legs feel sticky as if they have minds of their own.

Ron's hands and feet start to tap, quietly at first before getting louder and louder until his teacher taps him and whispers, "Ron, do you remember the way to help control your body we talked about?"
Which one? Ron wonders, the wiggly feeling making him feel that he is about to burst.

Have you ever felt like Ron? I sure have. Wiggle your left thumb if you've felt that way. I'll bet you have, even if you aren't wiggling it. How do I know? I'm Self-Control, remember? I just know these things!

Ready to help? Great! The superpower we are about to try is called **Push Your Wiggles!** Scoop up all the wiggles in your body. Start at your toes and go all the way up to your head. Hold them in your hands. Do you have all of them? Great.

Now, here's where it gets a little tricky. Pay close attention. Cross one arm over the other arm, so that your hands are on your shoulders. Your hands need to be closed and holding your wiggles. Now, open up your hands and push down on your shoulders, making those wiggles disappear! Magic!

What do you think? Was our **Push Your Wiggles** exercise enough to help Ron sit and listen to his teacher? Let's find out...

Go, Ron! **Push Your Wiggles** was just the superpower Ron needed to help keep his body still and his mind focused on what the teacher was saying. Ron's heard all the teacher's words, and it sounds like today is going to be a really fun day!

SUPERPOWER #9: SQUEEZE YOUR WIGGLES!

Jessica is eating dinner with her family. Her sister, mother, and father are sitting at the table eating while they talk about their day. Jessica simply cannot sit any longer.

Suddenly Jessica is hanging upside down from her chair, attempting to stuff a piece of broccoli into her mouth. This isn't OK as she could choke if she's eating upside down! Jessica needs a helping hand so that she can finish her dinner.

Can I ask you a question? Do you ever have days where you feel like you sat for such a long time and didn't get to move enough? I sure have. Once, I went to a superhero convention that lasted for eight hours!

They only let us get up for 30 minutes! Imagine sitting for that long! I won't be going back there for a while, that's for sure—not even for the delicious free pizza!

OK, remember our Push Your Wiggles! superpower?

We're going to learn a new one where we don't push the wiggles, we squeeze them. Kind of like an orange that we are turning into juice. It's called **Squeeze Your Wiggles!**

Just like before, take all your wiggles, starting at your toes and going all the way to your head. Now, hold them in your fists. Have them? Raise your right foot when you do. Now, **squeeze** those wiggles in your hands until they disappear. Great job!

Do you think our **Squeeze Your Wiggles** superpower was enough to help Jessica eat her dinner safely? Let's find out...

Wow, nice work, Jessica! What a superpower when you need to be able to sit still. The next time I can't sit still at the table, I'll definitely try **Squeeze Your Wiggles**. It's perfect for when I'm hungry but finding it tricky to sit down.

SUPERPOWER #10: SQUASH YOUR WIGGLES!

Jack is at recess. He is climbing up the monkey bars. He is so high! He swings from one to the next. Wow! He spots a group of friends playing tag. He zooms over, joining in and darting quickly away from the tagger. He is so fast nobody can catch him!

"Ring," the bell sounds. Recess is over. One by one, Jack's friends leave the courtyard, grabbing their lunchboxes as they line up. But Jack just can't stop running around the now-empty courtyard. "You need to line up," the recess teacher says, walking over to him. "But I can't stop running!" Jack says. "I mean it!"

Do you like recess? Nah, I'll bet you really don't like that with all that playing and running around. You'd rather, um, eat Brussels sprouts. I'm not knocking Brussels sprouts, though, they are pretty delicious.

I'm kidding about the recess thing. Recess is so much fun, isn't it? Did you ever feel like you just never wanted to come

back inside, and just keep running and playing? Touch your left knee if you've felt that way. I sure have; but with me, it was flying, not running. Not to brag or anything.

Let's learn the superpower of **Squash Your Wiggles!** to help Jack feel calm after recess. Take all of your wiggles and energy, starting from your toes and going all the way up to your head. Do you have all of them? Great!

Now, hold them like a big ball of wiggles between your hands. Ready? Now, push your hands together and **squash**, **squash**, **squash** the wiggles until they are gone! You did it!

I have a good feeling about this one. Do you think our **Squash Your Wiggles** superpower helped Jack get back in line with his class? Let's turn the page and find out...

Go, Jack, go! You guys are getting better at using the superpowers than I am, and I'm an actual superhero! The next time you have lots of energy and wiggles and you can't stop, then **Squash Your Wiggles** is the perfect power.

Are you getting a little wiggly right now? If you are, why don't you try one of the superpowers we just learned?

- Push Your Wiggles!
- Squeeze Your Wiggles!
- Squash Your Wiggles!

Do you need some help remembering how to do these superpowers? That's OK, ask your helpful reader to remind you. They are super awesome and would love to help you.

SUPERPOWER #11: COCOON

Joel is sitting at the kitchen table. He knows he is supposed to be doing his reading homework, but it is so hard to just sit and work when his mom is watching TV, his brother is eating dinner next to him, and he can't even feel his body anymore!

Joel throws his book down and starts jumping up and down on the couch. He won't be able to finish his homework if he can't get back to his book. If he doesn't do his homework, he might get into trouble in class.

Do you have to do homework? Even if you don't, I'll bet you can understand the feeling of just not wanting to sit still.

Have you ever felt so wiggly or so tired that you couldn't even feel your body anymore? That's a hard question, I know. Take a minute to think about it. You may not even know the answer, and that's OK.

For this next superpower, we are going to need space on the floor. Get ready for our next superpower, **Cocoon**.

First, get on your hands and knees. Next, cradle your head in your arms and curl your body into a tight, tight ball. You can do this with your belly facing the floor, or to the side.

Now, picture where in your body you feel your wiggles the most. Do you feel them in your feet? Your arms? Your neck? Or are they all over your body? Now, squeeze those wiggles out of your body until they disappear. Ahhh ... so much better!

What do you think? Did we help Joel finish his reading homework? Let's turn the page and find out...

Hooray, Joel, you did it! Using the super-mega power of **Cocoon**, Joel was able to get back to his reading homework. And you know what, it's actually super interesting. It's a book about history, Joel's favorite subject! What's your favorite subject? Remember the **Cocoon** superpower is helpful when you need to concentrate.

CHAPTER 6

Anger Management

Woo-hoo! You are on your way, Self-Control superheroes in training! You are unstoppable, kids! This next one will be a cinch for you. Do you still have your cape and superhero mask? Great!

Next, we need to use our powers to help kids who feel **angry**. Do you know what "anger" means? When someone feels angry, they feel a warning inside that something is wrong.

When you are angry, you feel very, very, upset. Some part of you may even feel threatened. You can feel anger in your body and your mind. When you feel angry, your heart may beat fast, your muscles may feel tight, and your breathing may be fast, too. Your thoughts may be going too quickly!

Anger is a normal feeling and it happens to everyone. Even so, it would be great if we could learn ways to manage feeling angry so that we don't have to feel upset for very long.

Do you have a tip that has worked for you when you have felt this way? What made you feel better? If you feel comfortable sharing this, wave your right arm quietly. That will show the grownup reading this book that you want to talk about it.

SUPERPOWER #12:
STOP SIGN!

Class 1A is buzzing with the sounds of laughter, music, and happy talking. Jack and Lenny are stacking blocks to make a large and towering city. Everyone is having such fun—except for Melissa who is standing alone in the corner.

Melissa glances over to the center of the room. Aviva, Jack, and Ben are all dancing there, smiling and laughing together. "I'm such a bad dancer," Melissa thinks. "I can't go over there. Besides, they are having so much fun without me. They are just leaving me out. They don't even notice that I am all alone!"

OK, let's learn the next superpower! When you feel angry, you may just want to yell, scream, cry, or use your body in a way that may not be kind or safe. Guess what? This next superpower will help you to stop and get back in control!

Let's try it. This new superpower is called **Stop Sign!**

Close your eyes. Picture in your head your very own "Stop" sign. What colors does it contain? What shape is it? What does it feel like? Now, once you have it in your mind, tell yourself quietly: "Stop."

Do you know how to count to ten? Now, try counting slowly: one, two, three, four, five, six, seven, eight, nine, ten.

Great! Let's see if the strength of our **Stop Sign** superpower helped Melissa feel better. Turn the page...

Nice moves, Melissa! Looks like a super-smart move to use the **Stop Sign** superpower in this situation. Melissa calmed her anger and now she's having the best time with Aviva, Jack, and Ben. And you know what, she's made up the coolest dance in the class. And you can take my word for it, I'm a superhero!

I may be getting my vacation time earlier than I thought! Who knew you were such a fast learner? Are you sure that you didn't already go to Self-Control Superhero school? Yes? Hmmm, OK ... if you're sure ... remind me to find out what you eat for breakfast, then. It must be great for your brain. I should add it to my grocery list.

SUPERPOWER #13: MAKE A LIST!

Kingston did not clean up the toys in his room after playing with them this morning. "I'm sorry, honey, but we agreed that you can't go for the play date with Timothy until you've cleaned up your toys and made your bed up. And then we have to brush our teeth and wash our faces," his mom says.

"That's so mean! I'm tired! It's too much, I can't do it!" Kingston yells, flopping down onto his bed.

Have you ever had many different problems piling up all at once? When you get angry they all seem to come into your head at the same time and they build up. Wouldn't it feel better to get them out?

OK, let's learn the next superpower! It's called **Make a List!**

Close your eyes. Take a deep breath. Take a moment and think: Is there anything that is on my mind that is making me feel overwhelmed and angry?

Picture a paper and pen, pencil, crayon, or marker in your mind. Give a silent thumbs up when you've got it. Now, write or draw out each problem on that paper in your mind. Fold it up. You can always come back to it later if you still need it.

Great! Let's see if the strength of our **Make a List** superpower helped Kingston feel better. Turn the page...

Great job, Kingston! **Make a List** has really helped you sort out all the problems piling into your head at once. Using this power has helped Kingston think about them and then he was able to talk about them with his mom. Even better, they've come up with a plan for cleaning up his room. Wow, **Make a List** is a true superpower, isn't it?

CHAPTER 7

Emotional Regulation

All right, superhero-in-training! We are approaching graduation! You have mastered almost all of the superpowers! Can I call you when my alarm goes off? Perfect. Listen for my call, or watch for my fly-by. You rock!

All of the scenes that we are going to look at now have kids who feel what I like to call yucky feelings. Yep, you heard me right. I said yucky feelings, which are those bad, sad, mad, hurt, make-you-want-to-cry feelings.

Everybody gets them. But just like every other chapter of this book, guess what? There is something that we can do about them. That's where our superpowers come in!

Do you have a tip that has worked for you when you felt any of these yucky feelings? What made you feel better? If you feel comfortable sharing this, blink your eyes three times. That will show the grownup reading this book that you want to talk about it.

SUPERPOWER #14: TAKE YOURSELF TO A PEACEFUL PLACE INSIDE!

Maggie is very overwhelmed. Her friends in school did not want to sit with her during lunch, her teacher told her that she was not listening, and now her brother was touching the new slime that she had just got for her birthday!

It was just too much ... she pushed him! "That's mine!" Maggie yelled, grabbing the slime away from her brother

angrily. "Go to your room!" Maggie's mom exclaims. "We use our words, not our hands." Her hands in fists, shoulders hunched, she yells at her mother, "It's so not fair! You only see what I do ... he never gets in trouble!"

Here's a Self-Control fact: I have a little sister. Guess what? I always felt like she got away with everything, and I was the one who always got in trouble. This made me even angrier, which got me in trouble again, so I was in trouble a lot. Can you relate to this feeling? If you can, clap three times and touch your nose.

Time to learn one of our last superpowers: **Take Yourself to a Peaceful Place Inside!**

In between long super flights, and when I am feeling very overwhelmed, I sometimes take myself to an imaginary place, a beautiful place that is peaceful to me. It is sometimes a happy moment or a story that I retell myself. This is my favorite superpower! Let's try it!

Close your eyes. Breathe in and out slowly. Focus on hearing the sound of your breath going in and out. Now, that sound is going to take you to a magical place, a secret land called **Calmtopia**. Stretch out your arms. You are now floating, with twinkling stars above and below you. A shooting star passes by your eyes, casting a trail of glitter across your face.

Suddenly, a tunnel appears in the middle of the night sky, swirling purple, blue, and green, and you swim into it, feeling warm and cozy, as it gently pushes you onto a white fluffy cloud. It is soft and squishy, like a marshmallow. You sink into it, feeling cuddled and light. You are now in **Calmtopia**.

The sky is a sparkling blue, with little dancing rainbows scattered across the horizon. You can almost reach out and touch them! You realize that your cloud is slowly sinking, stopping at a bubbling brook surrounded by purple and blue flowers. They smell so sweet, you can almost taste them.

The grass feels so soft on your bare toes and fingers. When the clouds on the horizon clear, you see a silver-and-gold castle appear, with sparkling steps made from gemstones sprouting out of the ground in front of you.

You take a step, feeling the cool gemstones under your bare feet. You make your way to the castle. The old wooden doors open with a soft creak, and you cautiously step inside.

A room appears, its walls royal blue, a golden table in its center. A single note lies next to a jar of sparkling glitter on the table. The note reads:

Welcome to the Castle of Calm and Peace. Close your eyes. Picture in your mind all of the hopes and dreams that you have for yourself.

Now, open your eyes. How do you feel? Let's hope our new superpower, **Take Yourself to a Peaceful Place Inside**, helped Maggie. Turn the page and we will find out.

Wow. **Take Yourself to a Peaceful Place Inside** is truly magical. The most powerful, calming superpower I know. Great job, Maggie!

Just remember, remind yourself of this place and of those dreams that you made for yourself today. You may even find a speck of shooting star glitter left on your clothes.

Oh my goodness! We are now up to our very last superpower. I can't believe it. I can't wait to show it to you.

Let's help out our last kid in need for the day, shall we?

SUPERPOWER #15:
GIVE YOURSELF A HEAD MASSAGE!

Harry has been waiting for two whole weeks for his sleepover with Sam. They are watching a movie in comfy pajamas and eating snacks after regular bedtime. It's perfect.

Well, it's perfect until Harry's big brother comes and sits right between them. "Why are you watching this movie? Why don't you play catch instead? I'll start!" "Sure!" Sam replies, leaving Harry alone on the couch. "But I don't like catch," Harry says to them. "So you can watch the movie while we play, right, Sam?"

Tears well up in Harry's eyes. "This is the worst sleepover ever!" he thinks, going into his room and shutting the door. "They won't even notice that I went to bed."

Have you ever felt sad? Lonely? Left out? I have, and it doesn't feel nice. But guess what? There's something that we can do to change those feelings, even if we can't always change other people.

Want to know something to do with the yucky feelings we were just talking about? This brings us to our very last superpower, **Give Yourself a Head Massage!** Seriously.

Close your eyes. Picture where in your brain those yucky thoughts are. Touch your right knee with your left elbow when you've found those thoughts. Now, put your left hand on the left side of your head and your right hand on the right side of your head. Rub, rub, rub the yucky feelings out of your brain until they disappear. Amazing! And it feels nice, too.

I hope that we helped Harry turn that sleepover around! Let's find out.

And wouldn't you know it, Harry has done it! **Give Yourself a Head Massage** has worked a treat. This incredible superpower has calmed Harry down and rubbed those yucky feelings away. The best part? It's helped Harry be flexible, and when his brother and Sam came back, they were all able to play a game that everyone liked.

CHAPTER 8

You Made It, Kid!

Congratulations! You have earned the official "Self-Control graduation diploma!" Now that you have learned how to use my superpowers, I shouldn't be seeing you on my "self-control alarm watch," right?

Maybe one day, with enough practice, you can earn one of your own watches and become a full-time Self-Control Superhero. How can you do that? Like I said, practice, practice, practice. If enough kids practice self-control and use some of these cool superpowers, then I might be able to take it easy and share the superhero work with you!

I may even find the time to chow down on some take-out food on a Sunday, or pop by at your house, school, or even play date one day when you least expect me!

Self-Control to the rescue!

SC
OFFICIAL
SELF-
CONTROL
GRADUATION
DIPLOMA

PART 2

FOR ADULTS

CHAPTER 9

Using the Strategies in This Book

Activities in Part 2 that include a [download icon] have accompanying downloadable material that can be accessed at: www.jkp.com/catalogue/book/9781805017554

Take a Deep Breath

When I work with children, I find that using actual bubbles is a great way to give them a concrete way to see the right and wrong way to take a good, deep breath. Before reading this section, you can demonstrate yourself what happens when you breathe too hard, too fast, and with not enough air. Then, let the child have a turn.

To incorporate self-control into the activity, I like to say, "You may not pop the bubbles, just look at how beautiful they are as they fall," or "You can only pop the bubbles you blow, not anyone else's bubbles."

Make a Mantra

Some children may benefit from creating a visible tool, at least initially, that they can utilize daily, with a mantra that you would like them to internalize. This can be written/represented pictorially/visually on a bracelet, bookmark, post-it note, keyring, etc.

You can place the mantra in many places throughout the home and school settings so that the child can begin to internalize the message. They should be the one to choose the mantra to gain internal meaning and gratification from this strategy.

Use Your Words

Kids may have different reasons for not using their words when they are experiencing a strong emotion. This may be due to a developmental difficulty, a medical diagnosis, a learned behavior, or a combination of things.

Providing children with alternative ways to express themselves (e.g. a visual chart to express things such as "I feel..." or "I need..."), and allowing them to choose may be a good option. Providing them with an "I need a break" card when you are seeing warning signs that they are beginning to lose control is another strategy.

Creating a safe space in your house or classroom where they can take a moment to regroup (usually, pairing this with a visual timer is a good idea) will allow them to get their thoughts in order so that they can use their words, whether that is internal (thinking more clearly) or external (with you or another "helpful grownup"). Remember, using words is a difficult skill, and some children may need additional processing time for word retrieval.

Just Give Yourself a Hug

This is one of my favorite physical self-regulatory strategies from my first books, and a simple way for young children to get deep-pressure input on their own, relying less on adult intervention.

Deep-pressure, or proprioceptive input, provides the body with information about where it is in space and is a quick and simple way for a child to feel safe, comforted, and self-regulated. On that note, all children must receive regular deep-pressure and other sensory-based movement times throughout their day to stay regulated. This keeps their neurological systems, including their "cup of coping chemicals" in their brain, full and able to manage what daily life throws at them.

Whether you are a parent, teacher, or therapist, it is important to realize that children need the opportunity to engage in these opportunities and cannot be expected to sit and complete sedentary and often cognitive-based tasks without the opportunity for movement. Examples of types of movement are:

- Give Yourself a Hug.
- Cross Crawls.
- Jumping Jacks.

For detailed information on more movement breaks, you can check out my first book, *The Kids' Guide to Staying Awesome and In Control: Simple Stuff to Help Children Regulate their Emotions and Senses.*

Crumple Up Your Worries

To introduce this activity and make it more concrete, you may want to first complete the pencil-to-paper task, that is, take a marker and a piece of paper (providing the child with the opportunity of choice here as much as possible) and have them physically write or draw all of their worries. Once they are finished, allow them to actually crumple up the paper and throw it away. This process may help embed this superpower.

Throw Away Your Worries

You may want to complete a tangible activity before learning this specific superpower. For example, you may want to try utilizing soft physical items such as pompoms or cotton balls, having your child name each worry as they pick up each item. Next, have the child collect them all and throw these tangible worries away to a specified location of their choice.

As an alternative, you may want to do the following to go into more depth: Have them look around the room and ask them, "Where is a good place that you would want to throw away your worries? Where do you feel your worries the most? What color are your worries? Can you picture them in your mind?"

Have them draw a picture of themselves (full body) and, using different-colored crayons, markers, etc., have them draw the areas of their body where they feel their worries the most, and what color(s) those worries are.

Make a Worry Box

To make this superpower more tangible for some children, you may want to do an activity of creating an actual Worry Box. This could be a physical tool that is used throughout the day, or just as a preview to learning about this specific superpower.

Creating a Worry Box could be as simple as using an empty tissue box and decorating it with markers, or as complex as getting a wooden box from a crafts store and painting it and utilizing an actual small lock.

In terms of naming actual worries, you may either want to utilize small manipulatives, such as cotton balls or pompoms, or simply have the child picture the worries in their mind, as described in the book, and "place" them in the box.

Push Your Wiggles

When children engage in this activity, they are providing deep pressure to the body while also crossing the midline. This provides a calming effect on the nervous system and allows for the two hemispheres of the brain to "talk to each other," improving focus, as well.

Squeeze Your Wiggles

This is the same as Squash Your Wiggles but with different hand movements. To make this superpower more tangible, you can cut out squares of bubble wrap. Have the child hold one piece of bubble wrap in each hand. Explain that this represents their wiggles and that when they squeeze the bubble wrap, the wiggles will disappear! The audible popping noise should reinforce the message.

To differentiate this even further, you can purchase the large bubble wrap and have the child draw or write out a representative drawing on the bubble itself. Once they squeeze the bubble and it pops, what they drew or wrote will actually disappear.

Squash Your Wiggles

To make this superpower more tangible you can have the child take something small and squishy carefully between their palms such as a tomato, a peeled orange, etc. with their hands over a bin or a bucket. This can be quite fun but messy! Explain that this item represents their wiggles, and when they are squishing them, their wiggles turn into juice and disappear!

Cocoon

This is one of my favorite yoga positions that I often use in my clinical practice as a therapist. It is grounding, as much of the body touches the floor while the child is actively hugging and squeezing themselves into a ball, providing deep pressure throughout the body, with their eyes closed so that their attention is focused inward. This is a great gross motor and sensory integrative exercise to utilize before having a child sit for a prolonged period, or when a child is feeling extremely dysregulated.

Stop Sign

If you would like a more tangible way to remind the child of this important superpower, a good tool or strategy would be to simply sketch a stop sign. (Either you could do this or have the child complete this independently or contribute, which would provide ownership over the tool.) The stop sign should be small enough to fit on a keyring so that you can clip it to the child's belt loop as a reminder throughout their day.

Make a List

To introduce this activity and help to embed it, you may want to first complete the pencil-to-paper task. That is, take a marker and a piece of paper (providing the child with the opportunity of choice here as much as possible) and have them write or draw each problem that they have on their mind on that paper. Next, have them fold up the paper. Remind them that they can always come back to it later if they need to. This process may also make this superpower more concrete.

Take Yourself to a Peaceful Place Inside

This may be my favorite strategy in the entire book. In this particular section of the book, where Self-Control teaches children the superpower of Take Yourself to a Peaceful Place Inside, we are truly addressing the strategy of cognitive flexibility, imaginative thinking, as well as meditation, sustained attention, and mindfulness.

This can be as simple as thinking of a positive memory or using the Calmtopia meditation story as a script. If you read it routinely and consistently, it becomes a part of your child's "coping toolbox."

I work with a student, let's call her MJ. I have been doing many of these types of meditation stories with her at the end of our treatment sessions. One day, as she was leaving my office, she turned to me and said, "Ms. Lauren, you have to tell my mom about these stories. I woke up from a nightmare and instead of going into my mom's bed, I remembered the story you have been telling me, and I told it to myself and went back to bed!" Wow, what an "I-love-my-job" kind of moment. Tip: You can dim the lights and play very peaceful music in the background while you read the story.

Give Yourself a Head Massage

A way to make this superpower more concrete is to have the child first draw a self-portrait, with only the head and neck showing. Next, they should draw different thought bubbles coming from their head, sketching or writing out different yucky feelings about which they are thinking. Now, have them rub their temples and/or the top of their head. Finally, have them "X" out each yucky feeling as it disappears.

REMINDER BRACELETS

The bracelets on the next page will reinforce the 15 superpowers/strategies learned in this book. You can download the bracelets from www.jkp.com/catalogue/book/9781805017554. Children should wear them daily, with fading prompts from adults, which should, over time, transform these strategies into habits across different environments. The bracelets are divided according to the five sections in this book.

Directions

1. Download and cut out the strips.
2. Photocopy them to use them daily.
3. Option 2 (preferred): Laminate a bracelet and circle the preferred superpower that you or the child chooses. This creates a durable bracelet that the child can use daily.

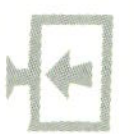

Frustration	 NO BIG DEAL! / I AM LOVED. / OH WELL, MAYBE NEXT TIME! / I AM AWESOME, NO MATTER WHAT! / I FEEL A LITTLE UPSET BECAUSE THAT WASN'T FAIR! / IT WAS MY TURN ON THE SLIDE!
Anxiety	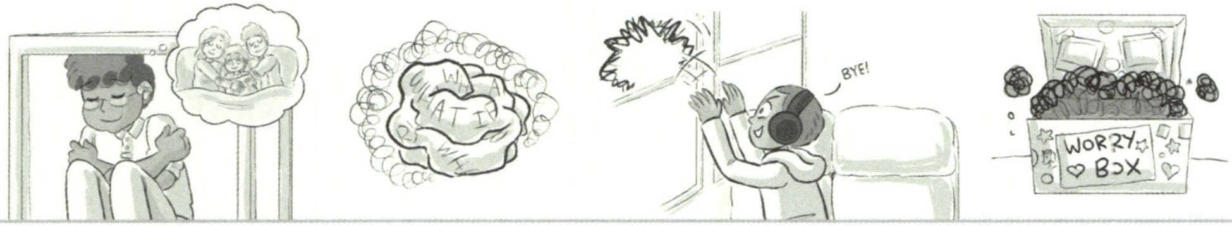 BYE! / WORRY BOX
Sensory Processing	
Anger Management	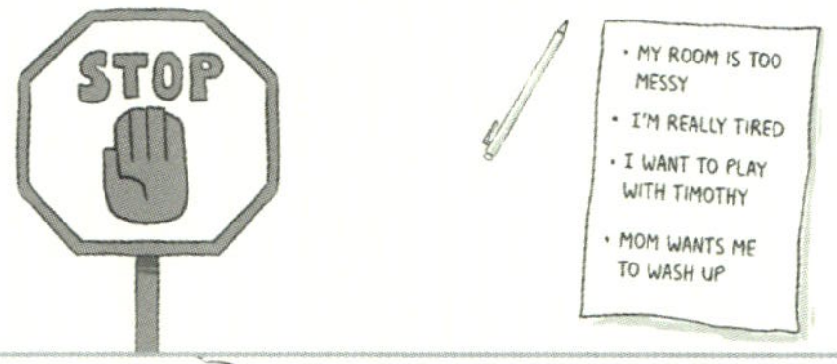 STOP / • MY ROOM IS TOO MESSY • I'M REALLY TIRED • I WANT TO PLAY WITH TIMOTHY • MOM WANTS ME TO WASH UP
Emotional Regulation	

SELF-CONTROL CERTIFICATE

CONGRATULATIONS!

You have mastered the superpower of

....

Date: ....

Adult signature: ....

Self-Control's Signature: ......Self-Control......

SELF-CONTROL DIPLOMA FOR KNOWING ALL 15 SUPERPOWERS!

CONGRATULATIONS!

ON GRADUATING FROM

Self-Control's Superhero School!

Date: ....

Adult signature: ....

Self-Control's Signature: ......Self-Control......

DESK STRIP/TABLE STRIP REMINDERS

These strips can be downloaded from www.jkp.com/catalogue/book/9781805017554 photocopied or laminated, and placed on a rug, at a desk/table, or on the wall, as a visual reminder of the 15 superpower strategies learned in this book. They are divided according to the five sections in this book.

FRUSTRATION

ANXIETY

SENSORY PROCESSING

ANGER MANAGEMENT	 STOP	 • MY ROOM IS TOO MESSY • I'M REALLY TIRED • I WANT TO PLAY WITH TIMOTHY • MOM WANTS ME TO WASH UP
EMOTIONAL REGULATION		

"AT A GLANCE" REMINDER CHARTS

These charts correspond to each key point (i.e. superpower) and address each physical or emotional state of regulation (geared toward children but accessible for adults). You can download the charts from www.jkp.com/catalogue/book/9781805017554.

FRUSTRATION

ANXIETY

ANGER MANAGEMENT

SENSORY PROCESSING

EMOTIONAL REGULATION

Acknowledgments

As always, I am so thankful to my commissioning editor, Sean Townsend, whose endless hard work, patience, and belief in the vision of this work has helped to develop it from an idea into the book that you are reading at this very moment. Words cannot express my gratitude. I also thank the amazing editorial staff and marketing team at Jessica Kingsley Publishers. I feel so blessed to work with a company that values the benefit of publishing books that make a difference in the lives of others.

To the parents and children with whom I have worked over the many years that I have practiced: You have been my teachers. I have learned so much, and I am blessed to continue to have so many of you in my life. To the parents, teachers, related service providers, and of course, children who I have not had the pleasure to meet (yet!): Know that I have been there, in so many ways. As a therapist and as a mom, I applaud you. You are amazing. Realize it each and every day.

To all of my amazing friends, near and far, thanks for the love and support. You rock.

To the love of my life, Joel: Thank you for tolerating the computer light in your face at all hours, my "I can't talk I'm writing," and for your continuous and unwavering love and support. You are my soul mate. Lastly, to my three little loves: You are my life. You are the reason I do it all. Realize that if you work hard enough, and want it hard enough, you can follow your dreams and accomplish more than you would have thought possible.

Dear Reader,

We'd love your attention for one more page to tell you about the crisis in children's reading, and what we can all do.

Studies have shown that reading for fun is the **single biggest predictor of a child's future life chances** – more than family circumstance, parents' educational background or income. It improves academic results, mental health, wealth, communication skills, ambition and happiness.[1]

The number of children reading for fun is in rapid decline. Young people have a lot of competition for their time. In 2024, 1 in 10 children and young people in the UK aged 5 to 18 did not own a single book at home.[2]

Hachette works extensively with schools, libraries and literacy charities, but here are some ways we can all raise more readers:

- Reading to children for just 10 minutes a day makes a difference
- Don't give up if children aren't regular readers – there will be books for them!
- Visit bookshops and libraries to get recommendations
- Encourage them to listen to audiobooks
- Support school libraries
- Give books as gifts

There's a lot more information about how to encourage children to read on our website: **www.RaisingReaders.co.uk**

Thank you for reading.

1 OECD, '21st-Century Readers: Developing Literacy Skills in a Digital World', 2021, https://www.oecd.org/en/publications/21st-century-readers_a83d84cb-en.html

2 National Literacy Trust, 'Book Ownership in 2024', November 2024, https://literacytrust.org.uk/research-services/research-reports/book-ownership-in-2024